1040 Taxes Could Be Replaced by One-Cent Fees!

Jeffrey Ross

Preface by David S. Jones, BA
With an Afterword by Jann M. Contento, PhD

Published by Rogue Phoenix Press
Copyright © 2018

Names, characters and incidents depicted in this book are products of the author's imagination or are used fictitiously. Any resemblance to actual events, locales, organizations, or persons, living or dead, is entirely coincidental and beyond the intent of the author or the publisher. No part of this book may be reproduced or transmitted in any form or by any means, electronic or mechanical, including photocopying, recording, or by any information storage and retrieval system, without permission in writing from the publisher.

ISBN: 978-1985646896

Credits
Cover Artist: Designs by Ms G
Editor: Arlo Young

Printed in the United States of America

Dedication

To the Memory of my Grandparents:

Dr. Ray H. and Virginia Reynolds
and
Samuel E. and Blanche M. Ross

Four wonderful people who taught me the value of a dollar.

Table of Contents

Preface
Introduction to the TFP System
Author's Qualifications
Basic Premise
Processing TFP: ACH, Software Platforms and Point of Sale Technology
Introduction to the Five Sectors
    Sector 1: Financial Transactions (Banking-related)
    Sector 2: US Equity Markets
    Sector 3: Energy
    Sector 4: Transportation
    Sector 5 Retail Sales
What Will Happen to Tax Preparers?
Form X: Income Verification, Rebate, and other Federal Program Certification Form
A One, A Two, A Three: Ways and Means and Fractions
Relationship to State and Local Income Taxes
What about other Payroll Deductions?
Implementing the TFP
What Must Happen to Make the TFP Part of American Life?
Arguments against the TFP
Cash Only Issues and the TFP
Consumption or Value Added Tax?
Fairness, Objectivity, and Privacy
Social Engineering
Final Thoughts
Appendix A
    Brief History of IRS
Appendix B
    Glossary
Afterword
References

Preface

The American people have long been recognized globally for their great ability to innovate and motivate change. For the most part, this creative mechanism has been consistent in our daily lives, except perhaps when we assess our most powerful government agency – the IRS.

Dr. Jeffrey Ross, a long-time English professor and published author, brings a unique and robust perspective to our current tired-- and tiered-- system of taxation.

His approach is fresh and fascinating. This book takes you through a detailed, yet simplistic, array of solutions designed to minimize and eventually eliminate the overwhelming stress we all feel during the pre- and post-tax season.

Ross is a pioneer. He shows no fear as he confronts this great challenge which faces our nation -- at the very least, his book will give you food for thought and, hopefully, promote a dialogue that will stimulate "the final revolution" for total tax reform.

David S. Jones, Sales Executive
BA, McGill University

Introduction to the TFP System

Since 1862, the Internal Revenue service has taxed personal income (of various types) to fund the federal government. (See Appendix A below for a brief history of the IRS). Each tax period has a certain flavor, so to speak, and the Code is typically reviewed, nuanced, and recast, but the information below succinctly describes the typical 1040 tax events and the massive numbers of individuals and amounts of money involved.

During fiscal year 2014, the IRS collected almost $3.1 trillion in federal revenue and processed almost 240 million returns. About 65 percent of all returns were filed electronically. Of the 147 million individual income tax returns filed, 84 percent were e-filed. Over 116 million individual income tax return filers received a tax refund, which totaled over $330 billion. The IRS examined less than 1 percent of all tax returns filed. About 3 percent of all individual tax returns examined resulted in additional refunds (IRS.gov).

Before the reader examines and analyzes the following text, you would be well served to jettison or dismiss whatever you think about the personal US income tax system. The accouterments of 1040 culture are so powerful, so intrinsically manifested in our society, it is difficult to imagine a world without refunds, credits, forms, the AMT, and tax season. My simple Google search generated 545,000 tax preparer hits in less than one second—and a similar search with key word phrase "tax software 2016" generated over 9 million sites. Look at all the money spent, and made, on the mechanics of 1040 culture!

The very subjective nature of tax preparation and filing should be considered, also. Take "your taxes," even the simplest of 1040 EZ situations, to five different preparers, and you may very well receive different interpretations and refund (or payment) amounts. (For an example of the subjective nature of tax accounting and preparation, see an article such as "A taxing challenge: Even experts can't agree when preparing a sample tax return" (2007).

My proposal provides for a general schematic which clearly demonstrates how 1040 tax revenue generation could be replaced by a simple and cost-sensitive transaction fee system.

The notions of flat tax rates, regressive tax systems, and even fairness will not be part of this book's working vocabulary. [See Appendix B below for a glossary of terms.] Tax reform is a popular topic among politicians and economists. With all due respect, most plans are only variations on the same old theme—income taxes. For example, Display 1 below contains basic outlines of the Rand Paul, Herman Cain, and November 2017 GOP Tax Reform plans.

> **Display 1**
>
> ### The Rand Paul Tax Plan
> Top Individual Tax Rate 14.5%.
> 14.5% value-added tax.
> Preserves mortgage and charity breaks on income tax and low-income credits.
> Businesses can deduct investments. (The Candidates, 2016)
>
> ### Herman Cain's 9-9-9 Tax Plan
> Nine-percent tax on personal income.
> Nine-percent tax on spending.
> Nine-percent tax on corporate income. No exceptions.
> (Herman Cain's, 2011)
>
> ### Highlights of GOP Tax Plan November 2017
> **Individual taxes:**
> Increases standard deduction from $6,350 to $12,000 for individuals and $12,700 to $24,000 for married couples.
> Individual tax rate brackets:
> 25 percent rate starting at $90,000 for married couples, $45,000 for individuals (everyone below that pays a 12 percent rate).
> 35 percent rate starting at $260,000 for married couples, $200,000 for individuals.
> 39.6 percent rate starting at $1 million for married couples, $500,000 for individuals.
> Expands the Child Tax Credit from $1,000 to $1,600 and provides a credit of $300 for each parent and non-child dependent.
> Makes no changes to deductions for charitable contributions.
> Elimination of student loan and medical expense deductions and the adoption tax credit.
> Doesn't change contribution rules for 401(k)s.
> Repeals the state and local tax deduction, but people can write off the cost of state and local property taxes up to $10,000.
> Repeals the Alternative Minimum Tax.
> Doubles the estate tax exemption immediately and repeals the tax in six years.
>
> **Business taxes:**
> Lowers corporate tax rate to 20% and lowers rate for pass-through entities (often small businesses that report taxes as individuals) to 25%. (Owens 2017)

Interested readers can find several flat tax plans detailed on the Internet. The new GOP plan is untested and complicated. Let's move forward. Tax brackets can be changed, exemptions modified, capital gains rates altered, and credits given. All such plans require exceptions, or have hidden agendas, or fall short of expectations. Flat tax or simplified tax plans within the existing 1040 system are only new coats of paint on an old wall, a barrier of confusion, misery, and inefficiency. And you would still be filing taxes with any flat tax plan.

When I mentioned to both friends (and family) I was working on a new plan to fund the federal treasury, resistance appeared from all sides. Several individuals decided I was un-American. One went so far as to say the idea was clearly a kind of nutcase thinking—the crazy product of those who want to turn America into Somalia or some other fourth-world country. Another panicky acquaintance bawled, "I don't want to lose my mortgage deductions! Don't give the government any ideas."

    As you will see, my friend would lose his deductions. But he also would no longer have thousands of dollars withheld from his paycheck every year. He wouldn't keep looking at the calendar to see how quickly April 15th was approaching. He would no longer need a shoebox to keep receipts—or a cabinet or safe to store paper work or flash drives—or schedule appointments with a paid tax preparer. And yes, I am trying desperately to give the government some ideas.

    Such a world without income taxes is nearly unfathomable. I have found it most difficult conversing about this proposal with almost everyone—they cannot discuss alternative plans to 1040 taxation without reverting to the vocabulary, the fabric, the images, and the tedious narratives of the tax system saturating our daily lives.

Author's Qualifications

Many have indicated I am not qualified to propose any changes to the American tax system. They point out sanctimoniously I am not an accountant, an economist, businessman, or politician. Thankfully, they are correct. I work part-time at a community college, I have co-authored books and articles about leadership and values, I am a musician, I am a trained ethnographer, and I have paid 1040 taxes for nearly 45 years. In my opinion, the current income tax system is too complicated, too nebulous, too subjective, and never pleasant. Here is Jason Russel's (2016) sobering description of the Tax Code's growth:

As they rush to file their taxes by April 18, Americans are rightfully frustrated with the complexity of the 74,608-page-long federal tax code. The federal tax code is 187 times longer than it was a century ago, per Wolters Kluwer, CCH, which has analyzed it since 1913. Amazingly, in the first 26 years of the federal income tax, the tax code only grew from 400 to 504 pages. Even through President Franklin Roosevelt's New Deal, the tax code was well under 1,000 pages. Changes during World War II made the length of the tax code balloon to 8,200 pages. Most of the growth in the tax code came in the past 30 years, growing from 26,300 pages in 1984 to nearly three times that length today.

The Code is a shapeshifter, an amoeba! Reid (2016) claims the only way we can straighten out the income tax situation is to start over: "The way to bring about fundamental change in a dysfunctional tax code is to start over — to rewrite from scratch." Perhaps tax attorneys, CPA's and politicians enjoy interpreting the code to those of us who are less informed, who must work for a living, and who live in daily fear of the IRS. Like most Americans, I am worn out hearing about tax brackets, exemptions, audits, wage garnishment, and how much tax the rich pay (or don't pay). I am tired of keeping receipts in a folder, struggling to find deductions, and getting filed-away paper messes together to do my taxes every new year.

Yes, my qualifications are perfect to proffer a plan.

As stated earlier, it is very difficult to let go of the archaic notions of withholding, itemization, deductions, and Schedule A's. The refund event is unbelievable. I am amazed American taxpayers are so happy to get a two or three-hundred-dollar refund—when thousands and thousands of dollars have been withheld from their paychecks for the entire year! Possibly some of you are convinced there is a moral obligation to pay taxes. In my opinion, morality or immorality has nothing to do with funding the government. My concern in this book is only how relatively painless mathematical efficiency can be applied to fund the Treasury. This proposal is about dollars and cents—especially the cents. And common sense!

Well-meaning folks have said my plan is unrealistic or unfair. As I will point out continually, fairness has nothing to do with this plan. I would challenge any of you to explain how the current system, the current Code, is fair—or consistent—or accurate—or simple. By the way, politics has nothing to do with this new proposal.

My new system for funding the US Treasury, The Transaction Fee Protocol (known hereafter as TFP) is based on mathematics, is not political, will generate sufficient funds, and is simple to articulate and conceptualize. Fully "automatic," the TFP will work because the software architecture already exists to support its implementation. Fantasy football, cash registers, ATM's, Amazon—all function daily using 21st century tracking technology.

This plan is not related to any state income tax, sales tax, property tax, Social Security tax, Medicare tax, or corporate income taxes—although the TFP will collect monies from corporations as well. (However, simple adjustments to TFP fees could also be used to potentially fund national health care, higher education, and Social Security. More on other possibilities later.)

This proposal moves forward from a very simple observation—1040 culture exists because the United States government taxes personal income to raise trillions of dollars to fund the federal treasury. The amount will undoubtedly increase in the future—but so will American commerce and the GDP. I have nothing against the IRS or the giant cottage industry populated by tax interpreting and preparing professionals. Unfortunately for tax preparers, many of their accounting services will no longer be needed within the TFP universe. This new plan will provide a valuable place for the IRS. (It will become the "New IRS," or "NIRS," under the TFP system—a purpose-focused agency explained below.) But the essential focus of this book will be how we can raise 3.5 or 5.0 or 6 trillion dollars efficiently and accurately while eliminating the unwieldy and often suspect 1040 tax return process. I am not concerned with the future careers of tax preparation professionals.

Basic Premise

A **trillion** is 1 followed by 12 zeros—**1,000,000,000,000**. This is, of course, a very large number. The TFP plan, basically, is to "automatically" assess a one-cent fee (.01 dollar) on all trackable transactions in the US (or those related international transactions using American financial institutions). To raise 4 trillion dollars assessing one-cent per transaction, 100 X 4,000,000,000,000 transactions will need to occur per annum. Is it possible? I believe so, and you will too.

I came upon this "idea" while examining electricity consumption by American homes.

According to the US Energy Information administration, the total sales of electricity to all sectors of consumers (residential, commercial, transportation, and industrial) was **3,758,992,000,000 kWh's** in 2015. Think of this—a one-dollar surcharge (or fee or tax) on each of the kWh's would have paid the 1040 tax bill for the entire country! Of course, no individual wants to pay such a fee. But what if fees were spread out into the network of electronic commerce?

What about a simple one-cent fee/charge on every financial transaction taking place within a calendar year? Billions and billions of transactions take place daily in the USA. I predict sufficient annual transactions occur in five major areas of the American economy to successfully replace the need for personal income taxes in the US (using the one-cent per transaction rate). These five sectors include ***Financial Services, Equity Markets, Energy, Retail Sales, and Transportation.***

Examples and statistics from each are described below. I will not provide exhaustive lists of transactions. The New IRS will be charged with finding, monitoring, and validating appropriate transactions—and setting up the processes for channeling TFP monies into the federal treasury.

But the proposal provides stunning documented figures, which clearly support the veracity and simplicity of this plan. As a side note, I might mention it is quite difficult to find simple count numbers describing transactions involving some aspects of our economy. Growth and economic numbers are typically reported as per cent changes or dollar amounts—not in customer counts or retail sales transactions. However, I will supply sufficient information to clearly articulate the evidence supporting these ideas—and whet the reader's appetite for absolute reform of the current federal personal income tax process.

Processing TFP: ACH, Software Platforms and Point of Sale Technology

      The software and network technology exists to enforce accounting and collection within the TFP. People consummate numerous successful financial transactions both online and at point-of-purchase sites each day. Numerous robust online accounting and book keeping software platforms exist, including (but not limited to) QuickBooks, Outright/GoDaddy Bookkeeping, Xero Accounting, Free Agent, A2X, and Inventory Labs. Software architecture now supports sales, payments, inventories, shipping, or payroll disbursement. Interested readers should study the products offered by Salesforce.com, Oracle, various Ecommerce platforms, and the myriads of accounting services provided by cloud computing. They exist and function successfully.

      And each of you reading this page is involved with some form of online transaction nearly every day.

      Think of McDonalds, the NASDAQ stock exchange, Amazon, gas stations, credit cards, debit cards, and thousands more electronic sales events. Dollars flow, salaries are paid, and taxes are collected!

      Two representative extant electronic financial "infrastructure" systems should be reviewed briefly to demonstrate America's technologically readiness to adapt the TFP. These two "platforms" are the ACH (Automatic Clearing House) system and Point of Sale (POS) software.

ACH

    According to Justin Pritchard, ACH payments are electronic payments made through the Automated Clearing House (ACH) Network. They are a popular alternative to paper checks and credit card payments because of the benefits to merchants and consumers: ACH payments are simply electronic transfers from one bank account to another. Look at any debit card statement, print or electronic, and you will see references to ACH activity. Common uses include:
1. A customer pays a service provider
2. An employer deposits money to an employee's account
3. A consumer moves funds from one bank to another
4. A business pays a supplier for products

Per NACHA (2016), "The ACH Network is at the center of American commerce, moving more than **$41 trillion** each year. That's made up of more than 24 billion electronic financial transactions, including Direct Deposit via ACH, Social Security and government benefits, electronic bill payments such as utility and mortgage payments, and person-to-person (P2P) and business-to-business (B2B) payments.

The ACH Network supports more than 20 percent of all electronic payments in the U.S." Think about this—ACH only supported 20 percent of all such payment transactions in 2016—there are another 80% to be discovered, tracked, analyzed, and counted!

Point of Sale Technology
"A point of sale system is a combination of software and hardware that allows merchants to take transactions and simplify key day-to-day business operations" (Crullon cited in Guinn n.d.). Essentially, POS technology includes a computerized check out network operated by a main computer and linked to several point of purchase (cash register-like) terminals including a host of features such as accounting, sales completion, inventory, and more….

All of us are familiar with Point of Sale technologies. POS is part of your daily shopping life. Think of computerized cash registers. They are "everywhere" now—from convenience marts to airports to department stores. One of the first microprocessor-controlled cash register systems was built by William Brobeck and Associates in 1974 for McDonald's Restaurants (POS n.d.). The systems function at all outlets where purchase transactions occur. Guinn (n.d.) notes modern systems can provide the following services:

- Inventory management
- Membership system
- Supplier recordkeeping
- Bookkeeping and accounting
- Issuing purchase orders
- Issuing quotations
- Stock transfers
- Barcode label creation
- Sale reporting
- Tax management and collection

Early systems such as the McDonalds cash registers mentioned earlier were site-specific. Modern POS devices can be connected easily via the web and cloud computing. The POS system would certainly allow for tracking and reporting TFP events.

In summary—ACH would allow for online financial event tracking, and POS would allow for tracking daily retail or what were traditionally "analog" payment events.

Introduction to the Five Sectors

Below, the reader will find simple data displays which contain information about significant transactions within five important economic areas. Included are **Financial Services, Equities Markets, Energy, Transportation, and Retail Sales**. The groupings are arbitrary and are not all-inclusive lists of providers or institutions. They are also limited in number and scope. For example, the Energy section only discusses electricity and gasoline, and the Retail Sales section barely scratches the surface of retailers and customers. Other sectors could have been added— Communications and Shipping come to mind—but the five discussed below provide sufficient examples of the numerous trackable transactions taking place continuously in the American economy.

Remember, all figures mentioned in the displays below, whether numbers in the millions, billions, or trillions, represent a transaction event during which a one-cent fee would be assessed to fund the US Treasury. Dollar amounts in themselves are not significant. For example, if there are **50 million** fast food customers a day, that represents **50 million** one-cent assessments.

My belief is that the sheer bulk of electronic monetary transactions each year will generate trillions of dollars—one cent at a time.

These transactions are merely representative—a very small slice of the American financial transaction pie. But significant numbers of daily transaction events take place in the five sectors described below.

Sector 1: Financial Transactions (Banking-related)

At the heart of this proposal is the fact American financial transactions are easily tracked and reported. (Interestingly, the identity theft protection company Lifelock claims to monitor **one trillion** data points a day for activity (Lifelock, n.d.). The following bullet point information from a Federal Reserve Case Study (2013) below in Display 2 shows the staggering number of electronic transactions using cards, online ACH transfers, wire transfers, and ATM machines. Of course, within the parameters of the TFP funding systems, each of the transactions, payments, and transfers below would be assessed a one-cent fee. Think of the permutations possible to fund our government!

Display 2 **Payments using Alternative Payment Initiation Methods** (Federal Reserve Case Study 2013)
Secure online payments, including methods that prompt users to enter personal identification numbers (PINs) for debit cards into the computer or that redirect users to a trusted Internet payment website to complete the payment, totaled more than 1.8 billion in 2012.
More than **250.6 million mobile payments were** made using a mobile wallet application and 205.3 million person-to-person or money transfer payments in 2012.
There were 287.5 million wire transfers—including those sent over large-value funds transfer systems and those made on the books of depository institutions—in 2012.
Cash Withdrawals and Deposits ATM withdrawals (**5.8** billion) in 2012 exceeded the number of over-the-counter cash withdrawals (2.1 billion) at depository institution branches At 1.63 billion transactions in 2012, over-the-counter cash deposit was the most common type of cash deposit, followed by ATM cash deposit, with more than 1 billion transactions.
Payment Accounts In 2012, there were 287.4 million consumer transaction accounts and 32.6 million business transaction accounts. Meanwhile, there were 279.7 million consumer credit card accounts and 28.5 million business credit card accounts. There were 775.4 million general-purpose cards in force in 2012
Card-Present and Card-Not-Present Payments Payments initiated when the card is read by a terminal are called card-present payments. In 2012, there were far more card-present payments by debit card (41.4 billion) than by general purpose credit card (18.0 billion) or general-purpose prepaid card (2.7 billion) The total value of general-purpose card-present payments was $2.7 trillion. There were almost as many card-not-present payments by debit card (5.5 billion) as by general-purpose credit card (5.8 billion) in 2012
[Notice the information above does not include escrow disbursements, cashier's checks, money orders, mortgage payments, or individual checks cleared.]

In related fashion… PayPal (n.d.) has become the global leader in processing online payments: In the second quarter of 2017, the company's net payment volume amounted to 106.44 billion U.S. dollars, representing a 23 percent year-on-year growth. This payment volume was generated through the 1.73 billion transactions which PayPal processed during that quarter. (In 2016, the payment provider's annual payment volume amounted to 354 billion U.S. dollars.)

Sector 2: US Equity Markets

Senator Bernie Sanders (I-Vermont) has long contended an "appropriate" transaction tax on Wall Street could fund American higher education. Carney (2016) wrote,

> Mr. Sanders wants to use funds raised by this tax to pay for his college-education agenda, which includes making public colleges free, cutting interest rates on student loans and increasing financial aid. The costs of these proposals—$75 billion per year by Mr. Sanders's count—could be fully paid by the tax. Investors would be required to pay an excise tax on any transfer of a stock, bond, partnership interest or derivative. Stock trades would incur a 0.5% tax rate, or $5 for every $1000 of stocks traded. Bond trading gets a 0.10% tax rate. Derivatives a 0.005% tax rate. Although those tax rates seem quite small, in theory they could raise quite a lot of revenue because of the size of U.S. financial markets. The total dollar value of U.S. stocks is around $25 trillion and more than $300 billion in shares is traded on a typical day. The bond market is even bigger, with nearly $730 billion trading on an average day last year.

Mr. Sanders' bill did not become law. (Although his ideas are still being discussed as this is written in November 2017). I sense the components of his proposal are too complicated. But I like the 'spirit' of his idea—especially since he understands the massive scope of equities market transactions. I am not interested in specifically targeting a demographic (the wealthy, in his proposal's case). No part of my plan should be associated with any sort of "Robin Hood" financial transaction tax—like the kind proposed by Hunter Logan in 1998 (Blue & Green, 2015). I am only interested in large-volume (not dollar amount) transactions—and ubiquitous, relentless, faceless one-cent fees.

The number of stock exchange transactions (trades) daily is amazing. Display 3 below shows trades and volume from the NYSE (just one of American stock exchanges) during the last three weeks of December 2016.

Display 3 Daily Summaries - National Market Volume Summary

Three Weeks in December 2016

Trade Date NYSE Trades NYSE Volume

30 Dec 2016   2,236,200   1,072,918,860

29 Dec 2016   2,002,287   717,384,705

28 Dec 2016   2,073,890   753,931,247

27 Dec 2016   1,686,277   605,171,142

23 Dec 2016   1,720,689   633,487,282

22 Dec 2016   2,358,073   903,626,946

21 Dec 2016   2,252,437   869,847,234

20 Dec 2016   2,531,828   991,075,200

19 Dec 2016   2,718,504   973,134,612

16 Dec 2016   3,308,693   3,317,849,390

15 Dec 2016   3,291,709   1,226,295,082

14 Dec 2016   3,588,974   1,277,189,539

13 Dec 2016   3,089,375   1,106,949,242

12 Dec 2016   3,193,030   1,205,936,403

(NYSE Market Summary, 2017, Jan 2.)

Display 4 shows composite trade data for one year from the NASDAQ. Such activity represents a fertile source for the one-cent TFP, whether assessed on group trades, block trades, or individual shares.

Display 4

**Nasdaq Monthly Summary
Volume for a One-Year Period 2015-2016**

Oct 16   7.97 Billion

Sep 16   9.63B

Aug 16   8.79B

Jul 16   8.01B

Jun 16   10.96B

May 16   9.21B

Apr 16   8.82B

Mar 16   10.06B

Feb 16   10.51B

Jan 16   10.70B

Dec 15   9.86B

Nov 15   8.40B

(Investing.com, 2017, Jan 3)

Other American stock and commodity exchanges [some of which are affiliated or have been affiliated with the NYSE and NASDAQ] are listed below:

- American Stock Exchange (AMEX)- Unlike Nasdaq and NYSE, AMEX focuses on Exchange Traded Funds (ETFs)
- Boston Stock Exchange (BSE) - This is made up of the Boston Equities Exchange (BEX) and the Boston Options Exchange (BOX)
- Chicago Board Options Exchange (CBOE)
- Chicago Board of Trade (CBOT) - CBOT is owned run by CME Group Inc.

- Chicago Mercantile Exchange (CME) - Owned and controlled by CME Group Inc.
- Chicago Stock Exchange (CHX)
- International Securities Exchange (ISE) - This includes ISE Options Exchange and the ISE Stock Exchange
- Miami Stock Exchange (MS4X)
- National Stock Exchange (NSX)
- Philadelphia Stock Exchange (PHLX) (Security Markets US, n.d.)

According to Silverblatt (2013), 7,238 mutual funds were available to investors in the United States back in 2012. In mid-2015, an estimated 91 million *individual investors* owned mutual funds (2016 Investment, 2016). Think of all the related fund purchases, capital gains distributions, dividend payments, statements, and other account services which could be assessed one-cent fees!

I would be remiss to forget mentioning High Frequency Trading (HFT). This is algorithm-based computer stock and bond trading that has gained in popularity and presence the last ten years or so. From *Investopedia*:

> High frequency trading is an automated trading platform used by large investment banks, hedge funds and institutional investors which utilizes powerful computers to transact a large number of orders at extremely high speeds. These high frequency trading platforms allow traders to execute millions of orders and scan multiple markets and exchanges in a matter of seconds, thus giving the institutions that use the platforms a huge advantage in the open market. ("What is High Frequency Trading?" n.d.)

Cheng (2017), writing about recent activity, notes that

> high-frequency trading accounted for 52 percent of May's average daily trading volume of about 6.73 billion shares, Tabb said. During the peak levels of high-frequency trading in 2009, about 61 percent of 9.8 billion of average daily shares traded were executed by high-frequency traders.

Again, HFT provides for ongoing, easily trackable opportunities for assessing one-cent TTP fees. Do you believe the stock market will become less automated, less dependent on computing? I do not.

Bond Markets

I cannot leave this section without making mention of the bond markets. Bonds are not equities: they are more accurately debt securities, and their actual transaction numbers are difficult to accurately report.

Seven main [bond] issuer categories exist:
1.) Treasury bonds;
2.) Other U.S. government bonds;
3.) Investment-grade corporate bonds (high quality);
4.) High-yield corporate bonds (low quality), also known as junk bonds;
5.) Foreign bonds;

6.) Mortgage-backed bonds; and
7.) Municipal bonds. (Stanton, 1998)

The volume of bond sales (and opportunities for TFP events) is far greater than stock market sales:

In the U.S. alone, bond markets make up almost $40 trillion in value, compared to less than $20 trillion for the domestic stock market....

Trading volume in bonds also dramatically exceeds stock market volume, with nearly $700 billion in bonds traded daily. That compares to about $200 billion per day in volume for stocks, per data from industry group SIFMA (Motley Fool, n.d.).

Hollwingsworth (2015) reports that "over the past 25 years, the bond market has been on average 79% larger than the stock market." But Hollingsworth also notes that bond sales are less transparent that stock market sales since so many informal secondary market sales and auctions take place. He indicates there is not a central location (like the NYSE or NASDAQ) that carefully monitors and reports bond sales. However, FINRA, a self-regulatory body with jurisdiction over many over the counter bond dealers, posts transaction prices for municipal and corporate bonds through a system called Trade Reporting and Compliance Engine. Even so, secondary bond market sales and associated fees are not as obvious or as trackable as stock market transactions. This is another area where significant TFP fees could be collected if such activities were more obvious and accessible. Creating protocols for such transparent transaction indices would be another part of the NIRS developmental mission.

So many other types of financial investments could be assessed a TFP fee—including derivatives, commercial paper exchanges, interest payments, and the many other transaction activities associated with financial markets.

Just so you know—In 2013, "Estimates of the face value of all derivatives outstanding top[ped] a **quadrillion** (1,000 trillion) dollars, or more than 14 times the entire world's annual GDP. By comparison, the total value of all the stocks trading on the New York Stock Exchange is roughly $15 trillion" (Sivy 2013).

Sector 3: Energy

Again, this is an area representing a virtual "mother lode" for transaction mining. Two areas only will be briefly examined—electricity and gasoline consumption.

Electricity consumption is listed in Display 5. Gasoline consumption is detailed in Display 6 below. I am not suggesting a surcharge on each gallon of gasoline or kWh of electricity. A payment at the pump—or utility bill—would each represent a one-cent TFP. But there are many ways electricity and energy are packaged, sold, and transported. Remember, electricity and fuel and other energy sources exist as salable commodities. Any paid transaction involving energy would represent a TFP event—whether wholesale or retail. The parsing of fees (on barrels or gallons) would be tied to a sales or trackable financial event market places populated by providers, middlemen, and distributors.

The facts and figures listed below merely represent a part of the breadth and volume the Energy sector represents within the Web of Commerce.

Display 5

Electricity Use
Total U.S. Electric Power Industry (in *million* kWh's)
Sales of Electricity to Ultimate Customers Sector

	2015	2014
Residential	1,404,096	1,407,208
Commercial	1,360,752	1,352,158
Industrial	986,508	997,576
Transportation	7,637	7,758
All Sectors	3,758,992	3,764,700 (these are trillion figures!)

(US Energy Information Administration, 2016)

Display 6

Energy Consumption (petroleum) million Barrels per day by year

Product	2014	2015	2016	2017 (Proj)
Motor Gasoline	8.92	9.18	9.31	9.37
Distillate Fuel Oil	4.04	4.00	3.88	3.94
Jet Fuel	1.47	1.55	1.61	1.60
Total	19.11	19.53	19.66	19.90

"In 2015, about 140.43 billion gallons (or about 3.34 billion barrels) of gasoline were consumed in the United States, a daily average of about 384.74 million gallons (or about 9.16 million barrels per day)" (US Energy information administration FAQ's, 2016).

Sector 4: Transportation

TFP's could be assessed in numerous ways in the transportation industry. A few significant statistics are listed in Display 7 below. Notice automobile, truck, and motorcycle registrations, insurance policies, license plate renewals, and related transactions are **not** mentioned. Keep thinking one-cent fee per transaction!

Display 7

Public Transit riders in the United States took 10.5 billion unlinked passenger trips in 2014 (DOT 2015).

Ridership on Amtrak has been growing since 2000, reaching a record 31 million passengers in fiscal year 2012 (DOT 2015.)

U.S. ferries carried an estimated 103 million passengers and just over 37 million vehicles in 2009 (DOT 2015).

The North American cruise industry embarked 17.6 million passengers in 2013 (DOT 2015).

Domestic and international passenger enplanements were 64.4 million in January 2015 (DOT 2015).

The TSA screened more than 432 million checked bags, more than 1.6 billion carry-on bags in 2015 (TSA n.d.).

Sector 5 Retail Sales

This is a very large segment of the US Economy—composed of 4.785 trillion dollars in sales in the United States in 2015 (eMarketer, 2016). There are many ways to "slice" the retail sales pie—the following examples listed in Display 8 are simply representative. Think of people buying a product or meal or service—and all the sub-processes related to such purchases—every day every, hour. Package delivery numbers are included in this section, although there are so many package and parcel deliveries such activities could be afforded their own section. The Display 8 list of representative customers and events related to retail sales could continue for several thousand, if not million, pages.

Display 8
Representative high-volume retail
   Fast Food customers.... Number served daily 50,000,000 (Fast food statistics, n.d.)
   Walmart 260 million customers worldwide per week. (Our Story Walmart, 2016)
   The U.S. convenience store industry alone serves nearly 160 million customers per day, and 58 billion customers every year. (National Association n.d.)
   Grocery Coupons Currently more than 3,000 companies issue over 300 billion coupons each year. About 8 billion of these coupons are redeemed. (Using Grocery n.d.)
   185 million smart phone users (Deloitte cited in Eadicicco 2015)

Package Deliveries
   United States Postal Service Deliveries
   By the Numbers 2015
154.2 billion — number of pieces processed and delivered
37 million — number of address changes processed
53.6 million — number of Click-N-Ship labels printed
93 million — number of money orders issued
5.4 million — number of passport applications the Postal Service accepted at post offices (USPS Fact Sheet 2016)

   UPS Average daily package volume 2016 (domestic)
1,379,000 Next Day Air
1,351,000 deferred
13,515,000 Ground (Selected Financial Data. (2016) UPS Press Room.

   Fed Ex delivers >
4 million packages daily (Fed Ex 2016)

   Representative Online activity (Kline 2016) follows....
Amazon has 244 million customers (at least one purchase in last 12 months)
In 2015, Fulfillment by Amazon shipped over one billion units on behalf of sellers.
eBay has 110 million active customers,
Apple has 800 million customers with iTunes accounts — 15,000 music downloads per minute in 2013 (Apple Press Info 2013)

   Costco Membership Data (as of 11/20/16):
87.3 million cardholders
47.9 million households
37.1 million Gold Star
7.3 million Business
3.5 million Business add-ons (Costco, n.d.)

By the way, in 2016 the total US trade with foreign countries was 4.9 trillion dollars. (Admadeo 2016). This includes $2.2 trillion in exports and $2.7 trillion in both goods and services. Again, actual transaction count numbers are difficult to locate, but think of the trackable fees, events, tariffs, insurance policies and shipping manifests Accountants among you will recognize the term Capital Accounts— those financial transactions that are all non-produced, non-financial assets. An example would be a Transfer of International Ownership such as a trademark or copyright (Amadeo 2016). They are measured by the Bureau of Economic Analysis—another potential partner for my proposed NIRS data miners.

Display 9 below contains suggestions for other transactions not mentioned directly in the five Sectors above which could be used for the TFP. Some of these may be retail in nature—some are not. The NIRS might parse these transactions in different ways, which could generate huge sums of money without being "noticeable" to consumers. Each of the financial matriculations below could carry a one-cent transaction fee. They are only suggestions—and meant to stimulate thinking about the many types of transactions which occur during daily life. Feel free to pencil in your own ideas!

Display 9

Higher education course registrations, costs per credit hours, carbon tax fees, utility bills, cable service bills, cell phone bills, vehicle license plates, drivers' licenses, toll roads and bridges, grain sales, EBT card payments, alimony payments, welfare checks wine imports, commercial fishing, natural gas thermal units consumed, hunting/fishing license transactions, prescription drugs, beer and spirit transactions, purchase orders, invoices, life and health insurance premiums, online newsletter subscriptions, medical board examination fees, apprenticeship exam fees, GED test fees, eBook downloads, music downloads, traffic fines, vending machines, food trucks, magazine subscriptions, satellite radio subscriptions, sports (like MLB, NBA, NFL, NHL, MLS) tickets, donations to charity, savings bond purchases, lawyers' fees, car rentals, subscription fees, title transfers, car warranty purchases, doctors' visits, lab tests, hospital visits, parking meters, lottery tickets, video game subscriptions, video game download extra packs, para-mutual wagering, golf games, slot machines, roulette wheels, casino poker, cell phone bills, cable TV bills, Internet bills, shipping containers, movie theatre tickets, arcade games, paint ball, laser tag, airsoft gas refills, HOA dues, union dues, state pension contributions/disbursement, building permits, hunting licenses, big game tags, emissions test fees, public school fees, youth sports fees, safety deposit box fees, Uber and Lyft fees, background checks, teaching certification, college sports tickets, skilled craftsmen services, examination fees, traffic violation fees, court costs, courier fees, mortgage payments, title company fees, PMI fees, fantasy football transactions, shipping lists, bill of lading, bill of materials, certificates of origin, parking meters, orders, invoices, manifest (transportation), railroad carloads, intermodal units, containers, cargo ship containers, title loans, credit union transactions, imports & exports, funeral services, building permits, sign permits, zoning inspections, monthly streaming or download subscriptions... .

What Will Happen to Tax Preparers?

As noted by IRS.gov, well over 1 million people have Current Preparer Tax Identification Numbers for 2017. See Display 10 below.

Display 10 **Number of Individuals with Current Preparer Tax Identification Numbers** **(PTINs) for 2017†**	741,124
Professional Credentials‡	
Attorneys	23,225
Certified Public Accountants	180,086
Enrolled Actuaries	292
Enrolled Agents	48,840
Enrolled Retirement Plan Agents	623
Other Qualifications	
Annual Filing Season Program Records of Completion Issued	25,365

† Cumulative number of individuals issued PTINs since 9/28/2010: 1,290,788
‡ Some preparers have multiple professional credentials and qualifications.
Page Last Reviewed or Updated: 03-Jan-2017

    If this plan is implemented, these Current Preparer folks will no longer be working on 1040 income tax preparation. They may be able to assist wage-earners with preparing Form X materials for income verification purposes (see next page for discussion), but the simplicity of the form will not create much of an industry for paid help. Hopefully, in the robust economy which develops post-1040, the former preparers can work with the NIRS or become financial advisors, long-term care advisors, stock brokers, health insurance brokers, or realtors.
    And there still may be areas of taxation—corporate, real estate, state income taxes—where they can help. I don't know what will happen to large corporate firms involved in tax preparation or tax mitigation.

Form X: Income Verification, Rebate, and other Federal Program Certification Form

This is only a draft (see Display 11 below) of what I now call Form X. I would recommend a 50-line maximum one-sheet for Form X. I mention this Form X idea cautiously—it is a link to the old system and must be articulated very carefully and simply. This form has one primary purpose: certifying income. Form X would be an optional document within the TFP system, but Form X would probably be necessary for most folks. Form X isn't related to taxation.

Many people would fill out Form X because the information within would demonstrate their eligibility for mortgages, car loans, student loans, health care subsidies, subsidized housing, school lunch programs, and the like—different but common kinds of activities for most folks. Form X would give individuals necessary income-level documentation (much like tax documents provide now) —and potentially provide the trigger for a Treasury rebate.

My preference is that lower income wage earners with larger households (perhaps as described by current poverty level guidelines) would receive fixed cash rebates from the US Treasury. The amount would be based on some actuarial principle or ratio of income and household members—clearly this could be developed to help those in economic need. The new "TFP Rebate Table" (replacing the 75000-page Tax Code), with a few rows and columns, would probably occupy a half page.

W2's, 1099's, capital gains forms, and dividends forms (along with all Social Security income and other income related paper work) would still be generated by employers and institutions to verify an individual's income level. (And to show state tax and FICA contributions.) And those income numbers could be reported on the Form X.

As I have mentioned, the TFP proposal is not about state income taxes, but this form could also be adopted for a common state income tax protocol.

Several of those folks who reviewed this manuscript indicated they did not like the use of any form within the new TFP system—any form, they say, would signal the return to more paper work, more complications, and a future cumbersome TFP Code. They may be correct. However, I submit this idea with the conviction people will need income verification paperwork for reasons cited above, and rebates could be given to those who meet specific and easily discernible mathematical guidelines. This latter rebate idea is a nod to "fairness" within the system, although I recommend it carefully and cautiously.

Is there a possibility of fraud or misrepresentation? Yes. Is there opportunity for criminal malfeasance now? Indeed. But I am recommending a very brief form—one that reports only income level and household members. Display 11 provides for a mock-up of such a form.

Display 11

(Draft) Form X for Income Verification Purposes)

Information
Your Name and SS # _____AGE___
Spouse name and SS #_____ AGE___
Mailing Address_____
Phone Number_____
Email Address_____
Over 65? Y N
Are you Blind? Y N

Income reported
W-2 _____
1099 DIV _____
1099 INT _____
1099 Misc. _____
Capital Gains _____
Rental Receipts_____
Game Show/Lottery Earnings_____
Other Net income _____
   Subtotal _____
Required Expenses
FICA Withholding_____
State Tax Paid_____
   Subtotal _____
Net Income total _____

Other Household members SS # _____AGE___
                                      SS # _____AGE___

A One, A Two, A Three: Ways and Means and Fractions

Throughout this text, I have referred to the use of a one-cent transaction fee. As described above, the fee would be paid by the initiator of the transaction. In other words, when a customer pays for his groceries at the market, a one-cent fee would be assessed by the **POS** checkout stand. The client who buys a fifty-share block of stock would pay a one-cent fee. But consider the much larger amounts of money which could be generated if a two-way fee were assessed, with both buyer and seller paying a one-cent transfer fee. I suppose such a two-way fee would be felt more sharply by the consumer. The banks might not appreciate paying a larger fee. But the possibilities for fundraising would be exciting. With a total two-cent transaction fee, the number of transactions required to fund the federal government would be cut in half!

Speaking of the one-cent TFP—why did I choose the penny as the nominal charge amount? Some of my colleagues sense a fractional amount would be sufficient to raise the cash needed to fund the government. But the quantitative and qualitative aspect of the one-cent charge is attractive. Fractional amounts would alter "simple" bookkeeping too much—how would .004 be recorded in a checking account ledger or online statement? Plus, the penny has a nicely iconic Americana feel to it: "A penny saved is a penny earned," piggybanks love them, and they seem to rest comfortably in bowls and coffee cans everywhere—never noticed as they hibernate and wait for someone to finally take them to a coin-changing machine at the local grocery store. Let's put those copper pennies to work in the TFP and make the US Treasury great again!

We could easily make a case for a two-cent or three-cent TFP, which would generate large sums of money with even simple one-way transactions. Consider the possible permutations and numbers with one or two-way transactions at three cents each way. Depending on government need, the structure of the TFP could be changed yearly.

Which brings me to a final point in this section. I began this book with the idea one-cent one-way transactions, in place of 1040 income taxes, could fund the federal treasury. And 1040 replacement is still the primary focus of this proposal. However, two-way transactions involving varying fee amounts, up to three cents, might fund two other social needs—education and health care. But that is a topic for a future book!

Relationship to State and Local Income Taxes

As indicated earlier, the TFP has only a potential—or future— connection to state and local income taxes. One step at a time! Surely a second penny, or some variation of transaction fees, could be used to fund state (and local) income taxes. It would seem a two-cent fee (total) TFP would be enough to fund federal and state treasuries, but the mechanics of the state TFP might involve more sophisticated software tracking systems. Surely such a system could be developed quickly also. The idea is appealing.

Alaska, Florida, Nevada, South Dakota, Texas, Washington and Wyoming do not have income taxes now. The implementation of the TFP plan might facilitate other states moving in the "income tax free" direction. The TFP would change the way states levy income taxes. And, as mentioned, this proposal would not recommend changing the current document process used to verify income (1099's, W-2's and others) at the state level, since these would be required still for income verification.

What about other Payroll Deductions?

At the risk of sounding redundant, other payroll taxes (FICA—Medicare and Social Security) could also be funded through a TFP enhancement. So could the reduction of our national debt. But for the time being, this proposal only deals with Federal income taxes.

Implementing the TFP

The TFP plan should be piloted or tested in retro-fashion initially. Equity markets, which are carefully structured and monitored by the Securities Exchange Commission, could provide an excellent test bed. A group of software/accounting people, and statisticians, could simply review archived stock and bond market transactions (including ETF and mutual fund activities, dividend payments, capital gains distributions) for any recent year. The total number of stock trades at all exchanges during 2014, for example, could be statistically examined to determine the actual funds amount of money which might have been generated for the treasury by using the TFP.

This same statistical process could be applied to the other previously mentioned sectors (and others) in the American economy as well. Surely the use of simple mathematics and prediction equations could quickly arrive at the feasibility of such a program as the TFP—and the pilot processes would undoubtedly uncover more transaction areas, which would help generate funds. Again, it would seem costs involved to develop such a pilot would be minimal. (Only millions of dollars!) The actual software program required to capture TFP fees would be relatively "pain-free" to develop and implement. Remember, all that happens is a simple one-cent fee is charged and directed to an appropriate US government account. There would be no inventory, shipping, purchasing, or customer satisfaction survey components to negotiate. No doubt the software engineers who support Amazon, Fantasy Football, and Google could develop the software package.

The mechanics of pilot and implementation seem doable. I am not so sure how difficult it would be to untangle the legislation and policy bureaucracy which supports the current system and its 75,000-page code. This 2017 period in American political history seems to hint at great change—and dissatisfaction with the status quo. So, perhaps the TFP's time has come.

I really can't imagine anyone complaining about a one-cent pay-as-you-go system.

Here is an important point! The TFP plan is meant to completely replace 1040 taxation, not to supplement the current system. I do not recommend the TFP as an auxiliary funding source. The TFP is designed to stand alone.

What Must Happen to Make the TFP Part of American Life?

1. Legal, political and policy issues must be approved. (Admittedly a huge roadblock to this plan!)
2. The system must be piloted—historically or retroactively at first to determine its feasibility.
3. Tracking and monitoring software must be developed and infused into the current electronic online systems (such as ACH and POS).
4. Oversight and accounting measures must be developed.
5. The IRS will morph into the New IRS—and become focused on systems rather than individuals. The old notions of enforcement— audits, liens, garnishment— will be outdated. The NIRS will need to develop mandates, techniques, and systems for finding and monitoring transactions and tracking compliance— and guaranteeing TFP funds find their way into the Federal Treasury. Surely, they will also need to develop penalties for certain non-compliant transaction situations. The NIRS will become a kind of TFP system-wide compliance accounting agency.
6. A brief "pilot" period of actual monitored transactions and fee collections will occur. In one scenario, the treasury could reach an agreement with a state to pilot the TFP for one year, and then return transaction fees to the state's general fund after the pilot.
7. Further pilot programs should be developed to assess feasibility of using the TFP system for funding higher education, Medicare, and Social Security.
8. A simple government website should be created which any individual can access to observe ongoing transaction accumulations and totals.
9. Let the transactions begin!

Arguments against the TFP

I have addressed many of the issues related to this new system. Critics, of course, will say the TFP can't be done. This new system of treasury funding would be an enormous change for our country. But the TFP is plausible because the models for its development and implementation already exist. America has the software and accounting systems to support such a plan. The financial transaction monitoring systems are already in place. Expert software engineers who work for successful online companies can fine-tune the platforms which support the TFP. Those folks who deal with the current every day complexities of online selling, investing, banking, tracking, shipping, and inventorying constantly strive to make the current online systems better, even though their systems are broadly effective now. Per Amazon founder and CEO, Jeff Bezos,

> Look inside a current textbook on software architecture, and you'll find few patterns that we don't apply at Amazon. We use high-performance transactions systems, complex rendering and object caching, workflow and queuing systems, business intelligence and data analytics, machine learning and pattern recognition, neural networks and probabilistic decision making, and a wide variety of other techniques.
> And while many of our systems are based on the latest in computer science research, this often hasn't been sufficient: our architects and engineers have had to advance research in directions that no academic had yet taken. Many of the problems we face have no textbook solutions, and so we — happily — invent new approaches… All the effort we put into technology might not matter that much if we kept technology off to the side in some sort of R&D department, but we don't take that approach. Technology infuses all our teams, all our processes, our decision-making, and our approach to innovation in each of our businesses. It is deeply integrated into everything we do. (Chaffee 2014)

~ * ~

Would retail or other purchases TFP costs be passed along by retailers? Maybe. But the cost will always be only one-cent. Buy a house—one-cent. Buy a candy bar—one-cent. You mustn't worry about percentages or brackets— the old way. Some will complain this TFP idea will place an unfair burden on the poor. Perhaps. But those who have more money (the wealthy) spend more money and enact more transactions. And as I have pointed out in several places, fairness in the sense of the old system has nothing to do with this proposal. The old system is not fair. Let it go.

Brokers and investment advisors who deal with equities might complain about a one-cent surcharge on individual share purchases (or blocks). But there will be no more capital gains taxes on the sale of any shares. Nor dividend taxes to pay. Ever. Again.

Financial planners may not like the idea tax-sheltered investments will become extinct. What is the use of an IRA, 403 B, 401K, or annuity if there are no taxes to pay? On the other hand, the business of "regular" investing should accelerate since more discretionary income will be available to investors! Tax-sheltered and tax-deferred investment vehicles are creations of the Code. They will be unnecessary in a Code-free universe.

International banking issues might arise. In today's global economy, numerous banks and accounts are used in the Web of Commerce. But the Web of Commerce is trackable and can be monitored for appropriate US TFP fee assessment. (Think of Amazon.)

Researchers and statisticians may not like the data provided in the five exemplar sectors above. That doesn't matter, either. I am using simple, easily recognizable examples and events which cannot be refuted. As mentioned earlier, I am only providing a few instances from the trillions of monetary interactions which take place in America. I am confident by now that you, the reader, get the idea. I am simply pointing out what can be done and illustrating, with accuracy, the financial transaction landscape as it exists today.

The biggest detractors of this new plan will be those who benefit from the current 1040 system status quo. (Yes, those who make money because everyone pays taxes!)

Cash Only Issues and the TFP

Some might recommend a black market would develop in the new fully-electronic **TFP** system as individuals try to avoid paying the one-cent transaction fee by using cash only. I sense many people within the current 1040 system already avoid paying income tax by getting paid "under the table" or accepting cash only for services—and not reporting such income to the IRS. Many taxpayers do not report all their non-1099 or W-2 income. And the dark money—from drug sales, prostitution, robberies, money laundering, protection money—I haven't heard of an IRS form for reporting such transactions.

With the TFP system, nearly all cash-only income, as it is spent, will eventually contribute to funding the US Treasury. Even garage sale earnings get spent somewhere! Because of the fully-automated system which utilizes POS, ACH, and other electronic systems, the fee will always be collected—when you spend your money. The 79-cent drink at the convenience store, paid for in cash or by card, becomes 80 cents. The 50,000-dollar automobile, paid for in cash, by card, or financed, becomes 50,000.01.

This system would also capture monies spent by illegal aliens and foreign visitors. Anyone buying merchandise at a POS register, or using a card connected to the ACH system, would be contributing.

The use of ACH-articulated sales and transfers will not decline in the 21st century. Very few Americans avoid the use of banks, credit cards, debit cards, and the like. Electronic transfer of funds has become the norm. The following information from the Fed Reserve (2014) *Payment Study* demonstrates the growth in debit card use—a common use of the ACH system:

> Overall, debit card payments grew from 8.3 billion payments in 2000 to 47.0 billion in 2012, increasing more than 3 billion payments per year, on average, during the period. While the rate of growth in debit card payments from 2000 to 2012 averaged 15.6 percent a year, the rate of growth from 2009 to 2012 dropped to 7.7 percent. The rise in debit card payments from 2009 to 2012, however, was also more than 3 billion payments per year. The diminished rate of growth in debit card payments during the latter period is thus not an indicator of diminished growth, but rather the result of debit card growth rates being calculated from a far larger base of payments in 2009 (37.5 billion) than in 2000 (8.3 billion).

And of course, when you pay cash for your tacos under the TFP system, the POS register will assess a one-cent fee.

The IRS nowadays seems quite comfortable with electronic fund transfers. More and more taxpayers are e-filing their returns. From IRS.gov (2014):

> As of March 28, the Internal Revenue Service has received 82 million returns through e-file—about 91 percent of returns filed this year. Only about 9 percent, 8.3 million returns, were filed on paper. The IRS expects to receive about 148 million individual income tax returns this year and projects that 23 million returns will be on paper, down 7 percent from last year's total of 25 million paper returns.

These passages serve to demonstrate most Americans are fully committed to electronic payment systems. Such trends will not be reversed. The IRS has faith in electronic payment articulations, something the NIRS will need to fully embrace. The Web of Commerce will only grow and become more symbiotic in future decades.

It would be very difficult to hide ACH and POS transactions since these two (and similar) platforms provide the support for much of American selling, buying, and banking.

Consumption or Value Added Tax?

Critics might suppose the TFP process is a consumption-tax—or a value-added tax. Call it what you want. But the TFP is different than the current 1040 income tax system primarily in that an individual is "taxed" on the "other" end of the personal income pipeline—after he receives his income—based on what he consumes. Those who enact more transactions pay more fees—but even these fees will be far less than the staggering dollar amounts required by the current tax bracket system.

Think of it—if a family of four was involved in 15,000 TFP transactions a year—their total bill would be 150 dollars. Can you beat that?

All interconnected transactions in the American economy will be fractionally contributing to the US treasury every second of every day. The Web of Commerce, the vast thriving field of purchases, fund movements, and fees, will provide monies to the federal government. And the corporations and financial institutions and retail industry—not individuals—will generate huge amounts of funds as they themselves continue to profit and thrive. In a sense, this plan proposes a movement from a personal income tax to a community-fee based system.

Even the government would be contributing to funding itself as federal employees, agencies, and departments make ACH transfers and buy goods through POS systems. True community funding!

Fairness, Objectivity, and Privacy

      The TFP system will be completely objective—no middlemen (including Congress, CPA's, tax attorneys, or software companies) will make decisions about your money and financial responsibilities. Those "professionals" with inside knowledge about tax deductions and credits will no longer be able to manipulate the system to their advantage. Within the current system, the rich can hire "better" accountants to find "better" tax-reducing loopholes. Such benefits for the wealthy will vanish.

      You might ask—how secure would such a methodology be? Well, how secure is the current banking and taxation and equity markets system? You do not dwell on this issue. You simply participate. Some might question the privacy issues related to ongoing one-cent fee transactions—but I do not see how this would be any more of a problem than current card and POS use creates. Current sales tax charges or fees do not create privacy issues for consumers. (Identity theft related to false 1040 form filings will also vanish.)

Social Engineering

Some might believe the current income tax system promotes a kind of successful social engineering (Ross, R. 2017). That is, folks are motivated by the current tax structure to make significant purchases which fulfill "positive" national economic or social goals. Just two examples should suffice. For one, solar tax credits apparently provide incentives to jump-start the important and emerging American solar industry. But the tax credit system may be benefiting the utility industry, the entities most resistant to the solar transition, as they make the industry more of a corporate enterprise. In fact, the complete tax credit narrative as it exists today is often motivated by lobbyists and special interest groups and does not assist the individuals the programs were intended to serve.

Perhaps more recognizable and widespread, attractive mortgage interest deductions supposedly encourage young people to buy homes and help stimulate the economy—and provide stability in their own lives. However, there are no guarantees home ownership is always an appropriate decision—look back to the 2008 housing crisis. [Interested persons might read "The History of the Mortgage Interest Deduction" (2006).] Many will not agree with me, but from a faux-libertarian point of view, I might ask—should the government be involved in manipulating personal economies, through deductions and credits, for what "They" perceive to be greater or social advancement outcomes? Should the government help winners and losers with the vast, complicated system of deductions, credits, and potential loopholes? Do you think people would stop buying homes or going to the doctor's office if they lost the tax deductions for those activities?

Now this may sound harsh, but consider the current tax "rewards" for large families, persons with disabilities, the elderly, or entities with tax-exempt status, or those who are sick or injured and have huge medical expenses. Ignore your communitarian spirit, your sense of good will, and you will see at least a semblance of government social engineering at work as they reward and penalize.

The government decides how your tax dollars are spent. There is no check-off list on the 1040 for where you would like your money to go. You are not able to direct your tax payment to the military, or education, or welfare, or health care. You have no input into the direction of the federal government and its budget. You fund the budget and its approved line items. That process will be altered somewhat within this new plan. The TFP system will not affect how the government spends our money, but it will change how the government influences you to spend your own income. Hopefully, a transparent personal economic neutrality will emerge in the new pay-as-you-go TFP system.

Final Thoughts

Why hasn't something like this been proposed before? I might point out the TFP is a plan which has only become possible during the last ten years or so. The technology did not exist to support it—or at least not to contextually satisfy the American public or government agencies. The proliferation of social media apps, online shopping, and the overall digital revolution makes this plan much more palatable to your typical tax-paying American and federal accountant.

I suppose there are many details that need to be worked out, especially in promotion and implementation of the TFP. Does the issue of fairness need more attention? And privacy? Should individuals be notified of their total fee payments for a given year—and would the amount influence their eligibility for a TFP rebate? They will have an ongoing record of their TFP's listed in their banking statements (just like any other ACH or POS transaction). The entire national TFP process could be tracked and reported—but with privacy issues maintained appropriately.

Americans are fascinated by discrete particulars—endless details about sports, finances, politics, retirement planning, medications—details which may seem important but detract from the actual quality of our lives in the here and now. The current 1040 system is a metaphor for our bizarre obsession with tension-generating clutter. A one-cent TFP would make America more stress-free and most likely more productive. Our American social and economic landscape will be changed forever. Think of it. No more withholding—no more filing. No more mortgage interest, medical, education, or child care deductions. None of these deductions would matter because there will be no tax obligation to offset.

Qualified and non-qualified designations for retirement plans, IRA's, and annuities will vanish. All the old sales pitches about "improving your tax situation" or "tax-free municipal bonds" or "deferring taxes until you are in a lower bracket" will become meaningless.

NIRS audits will be reserved for transaction systems—or government accounting procedures. No more forms, instructions, notices, or refunds. No more Federal Tax Day, extensions, or letters from the IRS.

I am stunned by the amount of nervous and counterproductive energy put into the current 1040 tax system. Tax breaks, deductions, brackets, protests, how-to-manuals—all for what? A problem with implementing my system is that 1040 culture is as much a part of American life as baseball, the Super Bowl, and Disneyland. Think of the anonymity, the freedom from anxiety, the quiet efficiency of the TFP system. Calls for reforming the Code are legion. But the Code should be abandoned. The Code is an unfair analog antique. This proposal shows how funding the federal treasury can be done effortlessly— and dare I say it— with potential for fairness.

The TFP is a workable, sensible plan. Display 12 below shows in basic side-by side-comparative form many of the characteristics of current 1040 taxation compared to the proposed TFP plan.

Display 12	**Comparing 1040 and TFP**
Current 1040 Income Tax System	Proposed TFP Treasury Funding System
IRS audits individuals	NIRS audits system
Subjective	Objective
Thousands of pages of Code, possible forms, instructions, and schedules	½ page Form X
Analog with some digital characteristics	Digital
Subject to Fraud and misrepresentation	Transparent and trackable
Not "Fair"	Not "Fair"
System based on income, withholding, exemptions, deductions, credits, interpretation.	System based on ongoing Web of Commerce one-cent transaction fees
Possible extra payment due by taxpayer April 15th	No extra payment due by taxpayer April 15th
Possible refund or and credits based on interpretation of tax form input	Possible rebate based on income verification and household size.
Tax Season, Deadlines, and Tax-payer Anxiety	24/7 Transaction fee process pay-as-you-go system. No taxpayer anxiety or manipulation.
Giant Tax Preparation Cottage Industry.	Automatic online system.
W-2s, 1099's, and other forms verify income for tax purposes	W-2s, 1099's, and other forms verify income for income verification purposes
Individual taxes support US Treasury	Web of Commerce transaction fees support US Treasury.
Ubiquitous Taxpayer Anxiety	No Taxpayers or Anxiety
Murky at best	Possibilities for complete transparency
Taxes income	Charges fee

Appendix A

Brief History of IRS
(courtesy IRS.gov)

The roots of IRS go back to the Civil War when President Lincoln and Congress, in 1862, created the position of commissioner of Internal Revenue and enacted an income tax to pay war expenses. The income tax was repealed 10 years later. Congress revived the income tax in 1894, but the Supreme Court ruled it unconstitutional the following year.

16th Amendment

In 1913, Wyoming ratified the 16th Amendment, providing the three-quarter majority of states necessary to amend the Constitution. The 16th Amendment gave Congress the authority to enact an income tax. That same year, the first Form 1040 appeared after Congress levied a 1 percent tax on net personal incomes above $3,000 with a 6 percent surtax on incomes of more than $500,000.

In 1918, during World War I, the top rate of the income tax rose to 77 percent to help finance the war effort. It dropped sharply in the post-war years, down to 24 percent in 1929, and rose again during the Depression. During World War II, Congress introduced payroll withholding and quarterly tax payments.

A New Name

In the fifties, the agency was reorganized to replace a patronage system with career, professional employees. The Bureau of Internal Revenue name was changed to the Internal Revenue Service. Only the IRS commissioner and chief counsel are selected by the president and confirmed by the Senate.

Today's IRS Organization

The IRS Restructuring and Reform Act of 1998 prompted the most comprehensive reorganization and modernization of IRS in nearly half a century. The IRS reorganized itself to closely resemble the private sector model of organizing around customers with similar needs.

Appendix B

Glossary

ACH: ACH payments are simply electronic transfers from one bank account to another

Cloud Accounting: Accounting software that is hosted on remote servers. It provides accounting capabilities to businesses in a fashion like the SaaS (Software as a Service) business model. Data is sent into "the cloud," where it is processed and returned to the user. (Definition courtesy *Webopedia*.com)

Code: The code is a federal document detailing the rules individuals and businesses must follow, in remitting a percentage of their incomes to the federal government (Definition courtesy *Investopedia.com*)

Consumption tax: A tax on the purchase of a good or service. Consumption taxes can take the form of sales taxes, tariffs, excise and other taxes on consumed goods and services. The term can also refer to a taxing system where people are taxed based on how much they consume rather than how much they add to the economy (income tax).

(Definition courtesy *Investopedia.com*)

Derivative: A contract between two or more parties whose value is based on an agreed-upon underlying financial asset, index or security. Common derivatives are forwards, futures, options, credit defaults, and swaps. (Definition courtesy *Investopedia.com*)

Excise taxes: Taxes paid when purchases are made on a specific good, such as gasoline. Excise taxes are often included in the price of the product. There are also excise taxes on activities, such as on wagering or on highway usage by trucks. (Definition courtesy IRS.gov)

Flat Tax: The system that is typically referred to as the "Flat Tax" arrives at a consumption base by taxing wages and salaries, but exempts investment income from taxation. You can think of it as a tax on all current consumption and saving, with no further tax on that what people saved in the future. It is close to the current income tax, but with Roth IRAs for all saving (and with no restrictions or penalties).

(Definition courtesy *Tax Foundation.com*)

Mutual Fund: A mutual fund is at its core a managed portfolio of stocks and/or bonds. You can think of a mutual fund as a company that brings together a large group of people and invests their money on their behalf in this portfolio. Each investor owns shares of the mutual fund, which represent a portion of its holdings. (Definition courtesy Investopedia.com)

New Internal Revenue Service [NIRS]: Name for the Internal Revenue Service as it morphs to function within the TFP system. The NIRS will be focused on monitoring transactions, developing software, and performing appropriate accounting within the TFP system. Audits and Enforcement will focus on system wide transactions, not on individual taxpayers.

Personal Income Tax: The current tax placed on income by the US Tax Code and paid through the 1040 income tax process.

Point of Sale Technology: A computerized check-out network operated by a main computer and linked to several point of purchase (cash register-like) terminals including a host of features such as accounting, sales completion, inventory, and more….

Regressive tax: A **tax** imposed in such a manner that the tax rate decreases as the amount subject to taxation increases. "Regressive" describes a distribution effect on income or expenditure, referring to the way the rate progresses from high to low, so that the average **tax** rate exceeds the marginal **tax** rate.
(Definition courtesy Wikipedia)

TFP Transfer Fee Protocol: A one-cent fee attached to all electronically trackable sales, transfers, and payments. A one-way TFP would be paid by the (buyer) payer only—A two-point TFP would be paid by both buyer and seller (both payer and recipient).

TFP rebate: Treasury funds returned to US citizens, based on their economic/dependent status, from TFP collections. This would require some sort of documentation as suggested by the Form X section in this book. The fixed rebates would be based on household size and income only. A very simple row and column table, perhaps based on accepted US Poverty Level guidelines, would determine rebate amounts.

1040 Culture: The manifestations, processes, and products related to the extant practice of taxing personal income in the United States. Includes tax forms, vocabulary, the Internal Revenue Service, 1040 forms and schedules, refunds, payments, brackets, and anxiety.

Value-Added Tax: A value-added tax (VAT) is a type of consumption tax placed on a product whenever value is added at a stage of production and at final sale. VAT is most often used in the European Union. The amount of VAT the user pays is the cost of the product, less any of the costs of materials used in the product that have already been taxed. (Definition courtesy *Investopedia.com*)

Web of Commerce: The electronically interconnected system of purchases, sales, transfers, and fees which can be monitored, analyzed, and assessed by the TFP system using cloud computing, POS systems, the Automated Clearing House (ACH) platform, and similar conduits.

Afterword

Jann M. Contento, PhD.

Is a world without income taxes fathomable?

Any form of taxation is most acceptable when it is understood by most and paid by all. Considering the abundance of tax reform policies entertained by politicians and economists, it is refreshing to view Ross' ambitious revenue-generating plan. A proposal claimed to be neither political nor fair, this plan reassures readers that funding the government through taxation should be absent of moral conscience. Through logical, curious, and bold ideas, Ross builds a satisfactory case for changing the nation's 1040-tax culture.

The mandate promoted by Ross is to simplify current tax complexity by offering a cost-sensitive transaction fee system. Applying automated mathematical efficiency to fund the Treasury, the author recommends known software architecture to support implementation of his revenue-generating plan. Network technology infrastructure includes systems such as the *Automatic Clearing House* and *Point of Sale* platforms.

Ross offers convincing examples and transaction data for five primary economic sectors: Financial Services, Equity Markets, Transportation, Energy, and Retail Sales. Each sector provides substantial revenue-generating potential with opportunities for "transaction events" resulting in billions [and hopefully trillions] -- all through a one-cent fee assessment.

Definitional clarity is essential in determining transactional application.

What is less clear is the definition of a "transaction event." The clarification of what constitutes an "event" worthy of a transaction will prove critical in the success of TFP as a revenue generator capable of replacing current income tax. Whether purchasing a surfboard or an ocean yacht, the same one-cent transaction fee applies. This penny notion raises questions when considering a multitude of transactions. The definition of a "transaction event" may not have equal relevance when applied to financial services, for instance, or a Point of Sale retail purchase. This exacerbates the idea of the 'new' IRS determining what is considered a transaction within a revenue generating formula.

Voluminous fees please…

The TFP event, defined as a single financial exchange at a given point-in-time for large-volume [not dollar amount] transactions, is plausible. One successful instance of revenue producing "fee" assessment is evidenced throughout the airline industry. Initially contrived to help neutralize rising fuel costs (evidently, a heavy suitcase negatively contributed to the jet's fuel mileage), small fees applied to weighty luggage proved profitable. (Interestingly, a return flight passenger who gained seven pounds during a short business trip flies without penalty, but adding one pound to a travel bag somehow warrants a costly fee!) Airlines soon discovered fresh and very assessable fee applications—including seating, boarding passes, carry-on baggage, drinks, snacks, meals, and blankets. Tacked on fees have found a permanent place in air travel.

Public education (including colleges and universities) continues to employ numerous so-called "activity fees" to help supplement instructional delivery and many "extracurricular" activities (i.e., lab access, theatre, band, and athletic participation, etc.). Colleges may boast "no tuition increases, even while adding fees that steadily contribute to rising college costs. The use of activity fees in public elementary and secondary schools continues to mitigate deficiencies in state and local funding appropriations. Designed for high volume transactions, Ross' conception of a small, fixed, silent, and reliable fee may be best suited for stabilizing revenue flow.

Point-in-time transactions

The energy sector offers some firm examples which illustrate the precarious nature of the TFP application of unique point-in-time transactions. Mining, extraction, refining, conversion, exothermic, photovoltaics, fission, fusion- measured in tons, kWh, barrels, gallons, etc.-- are all tied by the author to individual financial events. Multiple points in time in the energy production process may include numerous unique transaction fees. The TFP plan considers "any paid transaction involving energy represented as a TFP event, whether wholesale or retail, and any sales fees associated with marketplace 'trackable financial events' populated by providers, middlemen, and distributors." Such an assessed transaction fee, a trackable financial event within the manufacturing process, may function much like a value-added tax. The Value-added Tax, or VAT, common to Europe, is a concept where the "value" of an item or commodity is increased during individual stages of production or distribution.

This facet of TFP logic is of concern because "value-added" transaction events can tend to expand exponentially and add significantly to final costs. Such an ongoing process could contribute to inflationary price increases, causing a potential decrease in purchasing power for goods and services. This situation begets public uneasiness, particularly when one considers transaction fees are determined by an agency, or government, with an insatiable appetite, a hunger only quelled by steady revenue generated through "large-volume transactions and ubiquitous, relentless, <u>faceless</u> one-cent fees."

Defining Transportation sector transaction events also elicits various conflicting point-in-time considerations. And Point of Sale retail ventures may illuminate a confusing or inappropriate single play on a penny slot machine or penny gumball purchase as a separate and unique transaction (if such diminutive purchases still exist), effectively garnering an equal one-cent transaction fee. Within Equity markets, itemized transactions conducted through sheer volume, or quantity of exchanges, over a specific time-period, may successfully warrant a normalized one-cent transaction. Nevertheless, some clarity is further required to understand what Ross means by transaction events in the equities and bond markets. Are single-day stock market trades considered individual transaction events, or does one day of trading constitute a lone transaction? Do group trades, block trades, or individual shares all require or manifest a simple one-cent transaction fee event? How should these fees be parsed appropriately and successfully in the financial markets? Fundamental success for TFP's proposed implementation rests on a <u>clear and concise</u> definition of a transaction event.

1040 Tax Culture and TFP Equity

Focused on the historic static nature of 1040 income tax culture, current government revenue creation, through taxation, is based upon personal income. In the broadest sense, Ross' revenue-generating plan considers *transaction volume* rather than *individual income* as the primary U.S. Treasury revenue source. Is transaction volume income-based? Is the author's TFP conception merely an indirect consumption tax, or value-added tax? Does TFP impose an inequitable burden on lower income earners? Dissenters may formulate a position opposing the TFP plan on grounds of unfairness. Some might assume the notion that lower-income folks, those less affluent, will disproportionally pay the lion's share of the TFP one-cent fee.

Daily transaction events warranting a one-cent fee may function within some "hierarchy of consumption" based upon fixed or variable needs and wants. Lower wage earners may spend a higher percentage of their overall income on life's necessities, and similarly, on the proposed appropriate one-cent transaction fees. The economic sectors presented by the author-- energy, retail sales, and, to a lesser extent, financial services-- may absorb a good portion of lower wage earner's trackable transactions.

Participation in equity markets, however, varies considerably among income levels. According to a recent Gallup poll, just over half (52%) of Americans say they invest in stocks. Nearly one-quarter of those with incomes in 2007 between $30,000 and $74,000 no longer participated in the market by 2016. Middle-class adults younger than 35 are even less likely to invest (McCarthy, 2016). A 2015 Bankrate survey indicates that "a majority of Millennials, the generation of people between the ages of 18 and 34, do not invest in the stock market, which includes buying individual company stocks, bundles of stocks through mutual funds or exchange traded funds, and contributing to retirement accounts such as 401(k)s" (Cornfield, 2016).

A disproportional number of higher wage-earning Americans, those participating in equity markets, would fall within a larger scope of TFP fee obligation. Market volume summaries provided within the TFP proposal highlight the abundant transaction fee revenues dependent on equity market participants. Ross notes related mutual fund purchases, capital gains distributions, dividend payments, and various account services as recognized TFP derivation. Debt security and bond markets offer an additional healthy source of TFP revenue potential, almost exclusively supported by relatively wealthy market participants. Those most likely opposing the TFP plan on grounds of "unfairness" may be more affluent, higher income earners who disproportionately choose to participate in the equity markets. Public and private sector corporate and non-profit parties, including political market lobbyists, may also raise shrill, opposing voices.

Charitable Protocol

Replacing some aspects of the 1040 income tax culture with the TFP may foster unintended consequences, altering traditional economic and social behaviors. TFP's reduction or elimination of the tax-exemption, tax-deductible, tax-deferred, charitable features of 1040 culture may appear inherently unfair to many non-profits and to some tax saving incentivized philanthropists.

Consider "tax deductible/tax sheltered" contributions. How does one encourage "tax deferred" retirement savings without 401k or IRA income tax savings advantages? Human behavior economists suggest an employer or federal government incentive may encourage automatic enrollment in a retirement saving plan, ensuring employee contributions while retaining individual choice (Thaler & Sunstein, 2008). However, individual retirement savings incentives could be further diluted if TFP changes 1040 culture and successfully alters the motive for a tax deduction or shelter.

In the absence of traditional federal income tax filing, what opportunity or incentives exist for contributing to non-profit organizations? Philanthropic contributions, partially motivated by potential tax savings, would no longer be virtuous ventures. The National Center for Charitable Statistics-*Giving USA* estimates that *individual giving* amounted to $258.51 billion in 2014, accounting for 72 percent of all contributions received. Including corporations (5 percent), foundations (15 percent), and bequests (8 percent), annual giving in 2014 amounted to $358.38 billion. How much of these actions are primarily motivated by tax advantage elements of 1040 culture? Does implementation of an actualized TFP plan have the potential to expose idealized philanthropists? In 2015, the tax-exempt sector in the U.S. included approximately 1,521,052 charitable organizations and an estimated 316,532 congregations. "Sources of revenue for tax-exempt organizations in 2012 were program service revenues, including government contracts and fees (73%), contributions, gifts, & government grants (21%) and lastly, dues, special event income, rental income and net sales from goods (6%)" (National Philanthropic Trust, 2017).

Individuals must file IRS Form 1040 and itemize deductions on Schedule A to claim the charitable deduction. There is a limit to the amount of all charitable contributions allowed during a tax year, and total charitable deductions cannot exceed 50% of adjusted gross income). However, certain qualified conservation contributions are eligible for a higher limit (Friedberg, 2015). According to the most recent IRS data, for the 2013 tax year, only 30.1 percent of households chose to itemize their deductions (44 million returns). Lack of taxpayer participation with itemization may reflect overall tax filing frustration.

Tax payers may be sensing that the overall financial return resulting from the work put into itemizing and listing deductions is insignificant—or simply not worth the effort—because of the Code's limitations.

The nation's 1040-tax culture, altered by TFP's alternative revenue generating process, may also affect deductibility of mortgage interest payments. Thirty percent represents a minority of American households who itemize, and only those who itemize can take advantage of the mortgage interest-- a deduction that more often benefits the wealthy. Ike Brannon, of the Cato Institute and Capital Policy Analytics in Washington, argues, "… America's homeownership rate at roughly 62% shows less than half of all homeowners using the deduction…the larger the mortgage and the higher the tax bracket, the more valuable the deduction…" (Brannon, 2017). Who really loses and who really gains from TFP?

The paychecks of working Americans would still contain Federal deductions under TFP implementation. According to *The Tax Policy Center Urban Institute & Brookings Institute*, about 75 percent of American earners pay more in payroll taxes than in income taxes. Two separate FICA tax withholdings, Social Security and Medicare, will continue to be imposed on both employees and employers within the Ross TFP plan. Funding serves these federal programs by providing benefits for retirees, disabled people, and children of deceased workers. Current contribution rates for employers match those of employees: 6.2% Social Security Tax and 1.45% Medicare tax.

One's-Sense

Ross' TFP proposal provides samples of a proposed optional income verification document, retaining both W-2 and 1099 forms, and offers imaginative one, two, and three-way transaction fee options that would generate substantial revenue. Although he flirts with the potential of TFP applications for state income taxes, corporate, real estate, or supporting healthcare and education, his overall focus remains on addressing current Federal income taxes.

However, a reoccurring theme continues to direct this reader toward the need for a clearer, active definition of a transaction event.

The Transaction Fee Protocol Plan (TFP) is designed to "…automatically assess a one-cent fee on all trackable transactions in the US (or those related international transactions using American financial institutions) …to annually raise 4 trillion dollars…"
This seems quite simple, but could such a plan discourage US business transactions and encourage overseas economic activity and business location?

According to the proposed TFP plan, "the new IRS will be responsible for transaction identification, transaction verification, software development, and funding verification." This is quite frightening: Transaction events determined and defined by a government agency. Voluminous one-cent fees would be directed to a U.S. government account, and somehow find their way into the Federal Treasury…with "all interconnected transactions in the American economy fractionally contributing to the U.S. treasury every second of every day."

Good Gosh. Would the government agency responsible for funding the U.S. Treasury take liberties to expand government? Would lobbyists and special interest groups work to help define a transaction or a non-transaction, or discover loopholes? Will transaction fees be used to incentivize or disincentives commerce activities? Would government become more of a corporate enterprise? The simplicity of Ross' proposed plan exacts a steady one-cent fee across multiple revenue generating transactions. TFP's multiple transaction events fortify its capability and feasibility in producing adequate revenue. TFP is also plain, natural, and easy to understand. But can such an approach sustain the Government's steady requirement for revenue? Although individual income taxes are the major source of revenue, the Federal Government also receives revenue through social insurance taxes and contributions, excise taxes, trust funds, estate and gift taxes, and Customs duties. Additional earnings come from the Federal Reserve System's lending to financial institutions, fees for permits and regulatory and judicial services, and from gifts and contributions (U.S. Department of the Treasury). These large-volume transactions align with, and support, Ross' revenue generating TFP plan.

One may suspect that the money and budget managers in Congress, with their many subcommittees and discretionary appropriations, would prefer a tax revenue fee based on a *percent* rather than a *penny*. They may argue that such a process would enable them to "better manage" discretionary spending. Ross would most certainly disagree, and so will many readers of his proposed TFP plan.

The beauty of Ross' TFP concept and its applications lies in its challenges, especially in challenging readers to conceptualize cultural change. Initial impact questions lead to additional outcome questions. Ross' theoretical framework formulates a steady conviction while covering a great deal of territory. This is a very satisfying effort. Ross presents ambitious and bold ideas for changing the nation's 1040-tax culture by offering an alternative revenue generating process. His insightful, imaginative, and thought-provoking Transfer Fee Protocol proposal helps set the table for continuing the conversational debate. I enthusiastically anticipate much intellectual, and potentially contentious, impassioned discussion surrounding Ross' TFP conception.

References

Amadeo, K. (2016, July2). *US Imports and Exports: Components and Statistics.* Available: https://www.thebalance.com/u-s-imports-and-exports-components-and-statistics-3306270

Apple Press Info. (2013). *iTunes Store Sets New Record with 25 Billion Songs Sold.* Available: https://www.apple.com/pr/library/2013/02/06iTunes-Store-Sets-New-Record-with-25-Billion-Songs-Sold.html

Blue & Green Tomorrow. (2015). *Robin Hood Tax: Retrospective.* Available: http://blueandgreentomorrow.com/economy/robin-hood-tax-retrospective/

Brannon, I., in Will, G., H. (2017, April 28). One tax change that should be made-and certainly won't be. *The Washington Post.* Retrieved from https://www.washingtonpost.com/opinions/one-tax-change-that-should-be-made--and-certainly-wont/2017/04/28/1f8fcac2-2b82-11e7-b605-33413c691853_story.html?utm_term=.014f9c75dab1

The Candidates' Tax Plans. (2016). *Wall Street journal.* Available: http://graphics.wsj.com/elections/2016/candidates-tax-plans/

Carney, J. (2016). What would Bernie Sanders' Wall St. tax look like? *Market Watch.* Available: http://www.marketwatch.com/amp/story/guid/D445E464-1824-478B-8D43-7F36BD9367F8

Cheng, E. (2017). Just 10% of trading is regular stock picking, JPMorgan estimates. Available: https://www.cnbc.com/2017/06/13/death-of-the-human-investor-just-10-percent-of-trading-is-regular-stock-picking-jpmorgan-estimates.html

Chaffee, D. (2014). *Amazon's business strategy and revenue model: A history and 2014 Update.* Available: https://www.smartinsights.com/digital-marketing-strategy/online-business-revenue-models/amazon-case-study/

Cornfield, J., in Shekhtman, L. (2016, July). Why so few millennials invest in the stock market? *Christian Science Monitor* Retrieved from http://www.businessinsider.com/why-so-few-millennials-invest-in-the-stock-market-2016-7

Costco. (n.d.). *Corporate Profile.* Available: http://phx.corporate-ir.net/phoenix.zhtml?c=83830&p=irol-homeprofile

Department of Transportation Statistics. (2015). http://www.rita.dot.gov/bts/publications/passenger_travel_2015/chapter2

Eadicicco, L. (2015). Americans Check Their Phones 8 Billion Times a Day. *Time.* Available: http://time.com/4147614/smartphone-usage-us-2015/

eMarketer. (2016). *US Retail Sales to Near $5 Trillion in 2016.* Available: https://www.emarketer.com/Article/US-Retail-Sales-Near-5-Trillion-2016/1013368

Fast Food Statistics. (2016). *Statisticbrain.com.* Available: http://www.statisticbrain.com/fast-food-statistics/

Fed Ex Fact Sheet. (2016). Available http://about.van.fedex.com/our-story/company-structure/express-fact-sheet/

Federal Reserve Board. (2013). *The 2013 Federal Reserve Payments Study Recent and Long-Term Trends in the United States: 2000—2012 Detailed Report and Updated Data Release.* Available: https://www.frbservices.org/files/communications/pdf/general/2013_fed_res_paymt_study_detailed_rpt.pdf

Friedberg, B. A. (2015). Tips on Charitable Contributions: Limits and taxes. *Investopedia.* Retrieved from http://www.investopedia.com/articles/personal-finance/041315/tips-charitable-contributions-limits-and-taxes.asp

Giving USA 2015: The Annual Report on Philanthropy for the Year 2014 (Chicago: Giving USA Foundation, 2015), p. 26. Retrieved from http://nccs.urban.org/data-statistics/charitable-giving-america-some-facts-and-figures]. [https://givingusa.org/giving-usa-2015-press-release-giving-usa-americans-donated-an-estimated-358-38-billion-to-charity-in-2014-highest-total-in-reports-60-year-history/

Guinn, J. (n.d.). *What is a point of sale system?* Available: http://www.softwareadvice.com/resources/what-is-a-point-of-sale-system/

Herman Cain's 9-9-9 Tax Plan Is Incredible! (Literally). (2011) *Atlantic Monthly.* Available: https://www.theatlantic.com/business/archive/2011/10/herman-cains-9-9-9-tax-plan-is-incredible-literally/246588/

The History of the Mortgage Interest Deduction. (2006). *The Tax Foundation.* Available https://taxfoundation.org/history-mortgage-interest-deduction/

Hollingsworth, D. (February 2015). *The Bond Market: How it Works, or How It Doesn't.* Available: http://www.thirdway.org/report/the-bond-market-how-it-works-or-how-it-doesnt-

Investing.com. (2017 Jan 3). *NASDAQ Composite Historical Data.* (Available https://www.investing.com/indices/nasdaq-composite-historical-data

IRS.gov. (2017). [Various.] Available: www.irs.gov

Kline, D. (2016). *TMFDankline.* Available: http://my.fool.com/profile/TMFDankline/activity.aspx

Lifelock. (n.d.). *How Lifelock Works.* Available: https://www.lifelock.com/how-it-works/overview

McCarthy, J. (2016). Just over half of Americans own stocks, matched record low. *Gallup Daily Tracking.* Retrieved from http://www.gallup.com/poll/190883/half-americans-own-stocks-matching-record-low.aspx

Motley Fool. (n.d.). *5 Bond Market Facts You Need to Know.* Available: https://www.fool.com/knowledge-center/5-bond-market-facts-you-need-to-know.aspx

National Association for Convenience Stores. (n.d.). *Research/FactSheets.* http://www.nacsonline.com/Research/FactSheets/ScopeofIndustry/Pages/Convenience.aspx

National Automated Clearing House Association. [NACHA]. (2016). Available: https://www.nacha.org/ach-network/timeline

National Philanthropic Trust (2017). *Charitable Giving Statistics.* Retrieved from https://www.nptrust.org/philanthropic-resources/charitable-giving-statistics/

NYSE Market Summary. (2017, Jan 2.). Available: http://www.nyxdata.com/Data-Products/NYSE-Volume-Summary#318

Our Story — Walmart. (2017). Available: Corporate.walmart.com/our-story

Owens, C. (2017 Nov. 2). Here's what's in the GOP Tax Plan. *Axios*. Available: https://www.axios.com/heres-whats-in-the-gop-tax-plan-2505430314.html

PayPal Total Payment Volume. (n.d.) https://www.statista.com/statistics/277841/paypals-total-payment-volume/ Accessed Oct 4, 2017.

POS Systems. *Slashmyfees*. (2017). Available: https://www.slashmyfees.com/pos-system

Point of Sale System. (n.d.). *Small Business Encyclopedia*. Available: https://www.entrepreneur.com/encyclopedia/point-of-sale-pos-system

Pritchard, J. (2016). *How ACH payments work*. Available: https://www.thebalance.com/how-ach-payments-work-315441

Reid, T. R. (2016 November December). How to fix the tax mess. *The Saturday Evening Post*. Available: http://www.saturdayeveningpost.com/2017/11/01/in-the-magazine/fix-tax-mess.html

Ross, R. (2017). Social Engineering and Tax-Related Sustainability. Unpublished paper. Aurora, Nebraska.

Russel, J. (2016). *Look at how many pages are in the federal tax code*. Available: http://www.washingtonexaminer.com/look-at-how-many-pages-are-in-the-federal-tax-code/article/2563032

Security Markets US. (n.d.). Investopedia. Available http://www.investopedia.com/ask/answers/08/security-market-usa.asp

Selected Financial Data. (2016). *UPS Press Room*. Available: www.UPS.com

Silverblatt, R. (2013). Are there too many Mutual Funds? *US News & World Report* Available: http://money.usnews.com/money/personal-finance/mutual-funds/articles/2013/06/10/are-there-too-many-mutual-funds

Sivy, M. (2013). Why Derivatives May Be the Biggest Risk for the Global Economy. *TIME*. Available: http://business.time.com/2013/03/27/why-derivatives-may-be-the-biggest-risk-for-the-global-economy/

Stanton, E. (1998). Types of Bonds: 7 Bond Types Explained. *The Street*. Available: https://www.thestreet.com/story/229831/1/the-different-kinds-of-bonds.html

Tax Policy Center. (2016). Distribution of Federal Payroll and Income Taxes by Expanded Cash Income Percentile. Retrieved http://www.taxpolicycenter.org/taxvox/most-americans-pay-more-payroll-tax-income-tax

A taxing challenge: Even experts can't agree when preparing a sample tax return. (2007). *USA Today*. Available: http://usatoday30.usatoday.com/money/perfi/taxes/2007-03-25-tax-preparers-hypothetical_n.htm

Thaler, R. H., & Sunstein, C. R. (2008). *Nudge: improving decisions about health, wealth, and happiness*. Yale University Press.

Transportation Safety Administration. (n.d.). *TSA releases 2015 statistics*. Available:6 https://www.tsa.gov/news/releases/2016/01/21/tsa-releases-2015-statistics

2016 Investing Fact Book. (2016). Available: http://www.icifactbook.org/ch6/16_fb_ch6

Update. Available: http://www.smartinsights.com/digital-marketing-strategy/online-business-revenue-models/amazon-case-study/

UPS Fact Sheet. (2016). Available: https://pressroom.ups.com/

U.S. Department of the Treasury (2017). *Resource Center*. Retrieved from https://www.treasury.gov/resource-center/faqs/Budget/Pages/us-budget.aspx

US energy Information Administration. (2016). *Electricity*. Available:

http://www.eia.gov/electricity/annual/

US Energy information administration. (2016). *FAQ's*. Available:
https://www.eia.gov/tools/faqs/faq.cfm?id=23&t=10

Using Grocery Coupons Effectively. Neighborhood link. (n.d.). Available:
http://www.neighborhoodlink.com/article/Association/

Value-Added-Tax (VAT). *Investopedia*. Available:
http://www.investopedia.com/terms/v/valueaddedtax.asppl.aspx

What Is High Frequency Trading? (n.d.). Investopedia.
http://www.investopedia.com/ask/answers/09/high-frequency-trading.asp Accessed Oct. 4, 2017.

About the Author

Jeffrey Ross, who resides in Arizona, is a writer, rock musician, and former full-time community college teacher. He has had four "Views" pieces published on InsidehigherEd.com, has authored and co-authored several national and international op-ed articles on community college identity, purpose, and culture, and has recently published numerous parody poems and articles on the Cronk News higher education satire website. Ross co-authored the comic and critically acclaimed campus novel College Leadership Crisis: The Philip Dolly Affair (Rogue Phoenix Press, 2011). He also authored the romance parody Love in the RV Park: A Romance for Men (Rogue Phoenix Press, 2013), a nonfiction life history Silent Sonora (Rogue Phoenix Press 2015), and the mature romance The Auroran: Cold Front Redemption (Rogue Phoenix Press 2016).

VISIT OUR WEBSITE
FOR THE FULL INVENTORY
OF QUALITY BOOKS:

http://www.roguephoenixpress.com

Rogue Phoenix Press
Representing Excellence in Publishing

Quality trade paperbacks and downloads
in multiple formats,
in genres ranging from historical to contemporary romance, mystery and science fiction.
Visit the website then bookmark it.
We add new titles each month!

www.ingramcontent.com/pod-product-compliance
Lightning Source LLC
Chambersburg PA
CBHW062123220526
45471CB00010B/3860